Death is Not A Failure of Life

Memoir of a Death Doula

Helen Louise Epps Vining

New York | Los Angeles | London | Sydney

ISBN: 979-8-88581-237-5 Hardback
ISBN: 979-8-88581-238-2 Paperback
ISBN: 979-8-88581-239-9 eBook

Table of Contents

Prologue

by

Lamar Vining

There is something almost eerie about this book.

My mother wrote it to help strangers face death. She spent years reflecting on what she had learned from helping families let go of the people they loved. She believed those lessons might help others someday.

What she could never have imagined was that the person who would need those lessons most would be her own son.

This book was my mother's dream.

Helen Vining was not a hospice nurse, a minister, or someone who studied death professionally. She was a CPA by trade—driven, disciplined, and extraordinarily successful. She built a career that provided not only for herself but often served as the financial backbone for much of our extended family. She was the person people depended on when things became complicated or uncertain.

But alongside that practical and ambitious side of her life, she carried something else that was harder to define.

For reasons that even she sometimes struggled to explain, people naturally turned to her during the hardest moments of their lives. When someone was dying, when a family was struggling to accept the inevitable, my mother had a way of helping people find peace in a moment that usually brings fear.

Years later I realized there was a name for the role she had been playing for much of her life. Today people might describe what she was doing as the work of a Death Doula—someone who helps guide people and their families through the emotional process of dying.

She never set out to become one. It simply became something she did for people she loved.

Eventually she began to feel that what she had learned from those experiences might help others beyond her immediate circle. That idea slowly grew into the book you are now holding.

She worked on it with a publishing partner who had helped bring millions of copies of the Chicken Soup for the Soul books into the world. They met regularly, shaping her stories and the philosophy she had developed over a lifetime into something that could reach people she would never meet.

She talked about the book often. It was one of the few projects that seemed to excite her in a different way than the business success she had already achieved. This was something more personal—something she hoped might help people during the most difficult moments of their lives.

She never saw it finished.

About fourteen months ago my mother woke up not feeling well. By the end of that same day, she was gone.

She was only in her early sixties. There was no long illness, no gradual goodbye, and no time to prepare for what life would look like without her.

The timing of everything that followed made that loss even harder to process.

Just one week before she died, my two children—my daughter Myania and my son—had moved to Atlanta to live with their mother after years of complicated custody battles. Losing them from my daily life was already one of the hardest adjustments I had faced as a father.

Then, almost immediately afterward, I lost my mother as well.

My father, who everyone called Skip, had passed away unexpectedly about five years earlier while traveling in Italy during the COVID years. When my mother died, the two people who had anchored my life were suddenly both gone.

My mother and I had become especially close after my father's passing. For years we were the two adults who could rely on each other when life became complicated. I took her to many of her doctor appointments. We traveled together often. She loved to travel and had seen much of the world, and many of those trips were adventures we shared.

Her grandchildren were one of the great joys of her life. Myania, my oldest, is a remarkable young woman—beautiful, incredibly intelligent, and already setting her sights on becoming an engineer. My son is a gifted athlete with a passion for basketball. My mother adored them both. They were her only grandchildren, and she invested deeply in their futures.

The last conversations we had were not about death at all. In fact, one of the last things she told me was that I needed to find a wife.

That was her way—always looking forward, always thinking about what came next in life.

After she died, life did not slow down to allow time for grief.

Instead, it became more complicated.

Family conflicts that had existed quietly in the background surfaced into legal battles surrounding her estate, even though her trust clearly outlined her wishes. At the same time, I had to manage the practical responsibilities she left behind.

I cleared out the apartment she had been living in along the Detroit River while her home in Ann Arbor was being renovated after flood damage. That house sits on Lake Forest, in one of the most beautiful areas of Ann Arbor, on land she purchased and developed decades ago when the neighborhood was first being built. It had always been one of her proudest accomplishments.

The renovations included completing the lower level she had been transforming into a walkout Airbnb space overlooking the lake, complete with a steam room and private entrance. Finishing that project became one of the many things that had to be done while everything else in life felt uncertain.

I also had to help navigate the transition of her CPA practice and make sure an elderly client she had been caring for under power of attorney continued receiving the support she had provided for years.

And somewhere inside all of that, I had to decide what to do about the manuscript she had left behind.

When I first contacted the publisher she had been working with, he surprised me. Out of respect for her passing, he offered to return the money she had invested in the project and walk away from finishing the book.

But I knew my mother well enough to know that was not what she would have wanted.

This book mattered to her.

So, I told him to finish it.

At the time I thought I was simply honoring her dream.

What I didn't realize then was how much I would eventually need the book myself.

CHAPTER 1

Learning About Death

Helen was four years old when she planned her first funeral. Her brother, who was seven, didn't pay attention to her because she was, as he liked to say in his loudest voice, "You're just a silly girl."

But to Helen, it was the most meaningful thing she had done in her life, up to this point. She had been waiting for something "important" to happen to her. She knew about time and that there were 24 hours in a day which was 1440 minutes. Her grandpa told her that, and he was the wisest person she knew. He would show her his pocket watch, and they would wait while the second hand moved around and counted out a minute. It seemed to take forever, and she always lost patience after the second minute. She could not imagine more than a day or two if she had to count the minutes.

It was April, the beginning of Spring, when a small gray mouse started hanging out on her family's back porch. He was such a tiny little thing with no other little mousy to hang around with, and to her, he looked hungry.

She would crumble up one of her breakfast biscuits and dip it in honey before setting it out on a cracked saucer and place it just outside the door. When he realized that Helen always had something for him to eat, she knew he could tell that she loved him. He would wait for her every morning; an expectant look on his tiny little face. Once, he even allowed her to touch his paw. She marveled at the softness of his fur and his miniature toenails.

The days were soft and warm. Sometimes the sky filled with huge gray clouds, thunder booming through the sky. Rains drenched the earth, calling for the seeds of life in the ground to rise up to meet the golden rays of the sun after the storm. On those days, she could see her little friend hiding underneath the stairs waiting for the rain to stop. After the rain swept across the yard and into the next street, the clouds opened up and sunbeams lit up the steaming ground calling her outside to watch the plants grow. Helen could almost see them pushing out of the ground, eager to point their leaves and petals up to. Tiny purple pansies nodded their delicate heads at her as she knelt to sniff them. After the cold Michigan winter, her mom was happy to have her outside breathing the fresh spring air and staying out from under her feet.

Every day Helen chattered with her new friend about how pretty the flowers were and how nice the grass felt to sit in. And she would talk about what she was planning to do after she helped her mom by picking up her toys. She knew he understood what she was saying because he would look at her with his dark brown eyes, blink and twitch his silver whiskers. One of them was slightly bent which is why she started calling him Wacky Whiskers.

They were friends until the day she couldn't find him. He didn't come running when she placed his usual treat on the porch. Helen searched for him all morning. Finally, she crawled under the porch and found his little gray body in the back corner. She picked him up and his head lolled in her hand. He was still so soft but no longer warm. This was the first time she had to deal with the death of a loved one. Devastated, Helen ran crying, into the kitchen. It took her mother a while to find out what the problem was.

Helen's mother was a smart woman. She knew sorrow when she saw it and did not treat Helen like a hysterical child. She treated her like someone who has lost their best friend.

"Helen, this is just the cycle of life. Do you know how old this little mouse was? Maybe he was a grandpa mouse and lived out his days. And he had you to make him feel better at the end of his life."

Helen thought about this and for the first time in her life, she realized that maybe she actually helped the little gray mouse. The more she thought about it, she realized his bent whisker and the white hair around his face looked a little bit like her own grandfather.

"Oh mom," she wailed. "Is grandpa going to die?"

Her mother took her into her arms and said, "Yes, Helen. We all die at some point but not for years and years and years. Your grandpa has a lot of years left. You will be grown up when it is his time."

She held her precious daughter and said, "I have an idea. This is what we are going to do. Would you help me plan a funeral for your little friend?"

Helen wasn't exactly sure what a funeral was, but when her mother described what they would do to respect the little mouse, she agreed. They found an old cigar box for the coffin and filled it with purple tissue paper, Helen's favorite color. She wrapped his little body in some of the extra tissue paper, then she added a piece of biscuit with honey. She finished by tying a purple ribbon around the box and dug a small hole in the back corner of the yard. After placing his coffin in the hole, she scraped the dirt back over it and placed some purple pansies on top. "Sleep well Wacky Whiskers," she said to him. But Helen never stopped thinking that he wasn't really dead. There was too much life in her little friend. How could he just be gone. She didn't believe it for a second. If he couldn't die, maybe no one really died. These were deep thoughts for her, and she wasn't sure where they really came from, but she knew in her heart, she was right.

The rest of the summer Helen played with my friends and ran in and out of the sprinkler when the weather got too warm to do much of anything else. Her mother invited her friends over for barbecues and her brother shot hoops in the front driveway with his friends.

The whole family took a couple of day trips to Lake Erie. It was wonderful, listening to the serene, gentle lapping waves, and the calls of the lakeside birds. Helen loved walking on the beach, digging her toes into the sand and feeling the water on her skin. The sound of water helped to heal her sadness. There was something magical about water that filled her with a sense of healing.

Back home, just being outside with the birds, the flutter of colorful feathers and their bright black eyes looking for food helped her refocus on the natural rhythms of life. Brilliant gold and blue butterflies fluttered on the flowers in full bloom, next to the growing garden. The iridescent hummingbirds hovering outside her bedroom window alighting on red and pink blooms as they sucked up the sweetness of the nectar was another signal that life was always around her. Summer has its own energy, and it seemed Helen was aware of everything growing around here.

*   *   *

Helen started school that fall and learned what it was like to sit still in a stuffy room with lots of other kids. No more playing in the yard or digging in the dirt.

"You have to keep your clothes clean," scolded her mother when she saw the dirt on Helen's new yellow dress. "You don't want people to think I don't take care of you."

She had never before worried what people thought about her. That was another new concept. When she asked her teacher if that was important, she looked at Helen and said, "You must always care what people think about you. That helps you to stay good." Helen wasn't so sure she was right when she heard her answer. That seemed like a lot of time worrying about other people's opinions when she barely understood what her own feelings were about things.

After school, the best thing about fall were the deep piles of leaves fluttering on the ground underneath the trees. They were crunchy and soft at the same time but best of all, they were so beautiful, an explosion of golds and reds and easy to hide in. She played lots of games in the leaves with her friends in the neighborhood.

Helen's mother picked the squash from her garden and started canning and freezing the other vegetables so they would have plenty of homegrown food to eat when the snows came. Helen was learning about seasons and time was making more sense to her. Especially since she had to be in school at a certain time in the morning. She had never worried about time before. Now it was a constant irritant in her life. She found it difficult to keep track of, but she did keep thinking about life and wondering how much time was there in a life.

"Do the trees die when they lose their leaves?" she asked my mother.

"No sweetheart, they just get ready for the winter and let go of their leaves so that when the snow comes, they don't worry about keeping their leaves green."

"So, will Wacky Whiskers wake up in the spring?" Helen asked her. Still not convinced that he was gone forever.

"No, Wacky Whiskers is gone forever."

"But the trees leaves die and they come back." She was still trying to make sense of this life and death rhythm and was failing at making a connection.

"My friend in school said her grandpa died and came back when they took him to the hospital. If he can die and not really be dead, does that mean we don't have to die, just like the trees which come back in the spring didn't really die?"

That was the end of her conversation with her mother for a while about life and death. She wasn't prepared to have this discussion. "You are too young to think about these things," she said.

CHAPTER 2

Winter

The end of Fall and beginning of Winter brought on the bitter cold winds, the ice and the snow shining like diamonds on the streets and sidewalks and hanging off the dark bare branches of the trees. It slowed down the pace of life, and everyone prepared to stay warm and safe. It was time to pull out her mittens and boots and heavy winter coat and scarf. Helen's mother still had a hard time keeping her in the house, especially when it snowed. Helen always found something new to wonder at. She pulled out her small magnifying glass her grandfather had given her for her birthday and looked at the snowflakes that landed on her mittens. Her mother was right. They were all different. How could that be? There were so many of them. When she asked her mother she said, "There are millions of people on this earth and no two are exactly alike."

"But what about twins? Aren't they exactly alike?"

"There is always something different, even between twins," she explained.

Helen thought about this for a long time.

*   *   *

As Helen grew older, she became more aware of death. She had even finally dug up Wacky Whiskers in her back yard, just to doublecheck that he hadn't come back to life. All she found was the box filled with bones and a dried up carcass. His whiskers were still there and so were his little claws. It had been five years since she buried him, so he had plenty of time to emerge from his little coffin. This was a disappointment to Helen because she had never stopped thinking that Wacky Whiskers might come back to life like her friend's grandfather. But even that was a one-time event. He had passed on the next year from a heart attack.

That was another thing that didn't make sense to Helen. What was a heart attack? Wasn't the heart the center of love? How could it attack someone from the inside out? Now that was really scary.

Helen was developing a reputation as someone who seemed to understand death more than her friends. If they had questions, they came to her and asked her what she thought. At first Helen thought this was very sad, that everyone thought she had all the answers about something so dark as death. But she didn't really think death was dark. She knew it was only a beginning to another existence where pain was no longer a daily occurrence. She just *knew* that it was filled with light and love for those left behind. She never stopped to think how she knew. It was just within her.

It was interesting how it happened in so many ways, and it didn't seem to matter if the person was good or bad. What was sad was how it affected people. Some people accepted it and some people couldn't stop crying and some people hid in their room trying to pretend it never happened at all. But Helen had a gift. She could help her friends through these times, and they loved her for it.

Sometimes the ideas around life and death that flowed through Helen's mind, seemed so complex and important she had to write them down. She purchased a special journal at the five-and dime and made it her official place to share such feelings. After a while, it became her best friend and allowed her to save her advice and how she arrived at certain decisions.

Helen's Journal Entry

Human beings are parallel to the seasons. They are born, they grow, they make plans, they create and walk in purpose. They just keep waking up with all the things to do that they planned to do the night before and they enjoy the life they have made in this season. They are surely walking in the results of everything they have done, maybe doing it three or four times, but it is the season where their lives are on full display. It is noticeable who is feeling like, I *did good* and who is feeling the opposite.

It is the time for winter food, comfort food. It is time for everyone to be kind, time to think about spirituality, celebrate more evolved acts, and love what they hope will occur in this winter, holiday season. It can be cold wind, blizzards, accidents. Danger surrounds the winter, and the year ends with winter declared. As these seasons are so consistent, so is death.

Death has been underrated for all our lives. People only associate it with pain, loss, sadness, regrets, guilt, and recalibrating under duress and then they evaluate the person. Their life is like, what will be said, who will be most affected and then exactly what will the future look like for the person who exited this dimension and mostly those who mourn their absence.

CHAPTER 3

The Death of a Brother
and His Funeral

Helen was only fifteen when the police knocked on their door late one evening. As soon as her mother saw who was there, she froze, unable to invite them in. She started trembling. Just seeing the police in their crisp blue uniforms standing at her front door, told her it could only be another tragedy in a family filled with tragedies, but even she didn't know what it meant this time or who had been taken from them.

Helen immediately knew. She didn't even stop to think how she knew, she just did. She turned towards the stairs and saw her brother, Joe, bathed in white light as he stood on the bottom stop. He was dripping water, but strangely, the steps remained dry. She could see his lips move but couldn't hear him speak. His face was filled with sadness as he reached out to her and then he faded away.

Helen started sobbing uncontrollably.

Her mother turned and looked at Helen, then looked at the police and said, "It's my son, Joe, isn't it? What happened."

One of the police officers said, "We can't say for sure what happened until the investigation is finished but we are sure it is your son. We found his driver's license in his jacket. Someone called it in, a body floating in the river. We are sorry for your loss. Can somebody come down to the morgue in the morning to officially identify him?"

Helen's mother just nodded and said, "I will do it. I have to know."

Helen's brother had been her best friend. They shared a lot of family secrets, and he helped her get out of the way of her papa who wasn't always the most understanding of his precocious daughter. What was she going to do now? Joe had even said to her in a teasing way, that she had better be good to him because he wasn't going to be around forever. He knew something was going to happen and she thought he was just messing with her. In her heart, she also knew when she saw him walking down the street, arm in arm with that pretty, blond girl, that she would only lead to trouble.

Joe was eighteen years old, his life had barely begun. Helen had heard the racist catcalls when he was out in public with his girlfriend. Joe didn't respond to the hostility from those folks who could only see the color of his skin. But Helen knew for sure that he was drowned by some of those evil white folks.

* * *

After her mother returned from the morgue the next morning, she called Helen into the kitchen.

"Helen, you are now the oldest child in the family and people will be looking to you for guidance. That is the way it has always been in our family. The women handle the trauma and the grieving. The men get out the whiskey."

Helen's mother pulled her into a tight embrace. "Be careful, baby girl. Watch where you step and watch what you say."

Everyone in the family felt guilty, though they had nothing to do with it. They all felt they should somehow have known or more importantly, Helen should have known, because she was the one with the gift. That was a heavy load to bear for Helen. No one really said anything, but she could tell what they were thinking. How could she have ever known that the hate she saw in some people's eyes when they looked at her beautiful brother would lead to such a terrible outcome?

* * *

The Funeral

Preparing for Joe's funeral was as difficult as anything Helen had ever had to do. She was with her mother every step of the way. There were notices to be sent out to all of the relatives and an obituary to write for the paper.

"He was so much more than these few lines of text," she thought. His life had been so short that when Helen read it, it made her start sobbing again.

There was the casket to choose, the musicians to hire to play Joe's favorite songs, the funeral cards to design, the headstone for the cemetery to order, the hall for the celebration of life after the service, the catering to decide on.

"Celebration of life?" Helen thought. "How can I celebrate this loss of such a beautiful human being."

In Helen's community, the funeral is the place where most people can show their last act of kindness. Helen's people would be so invested in sending someone home nicely, meaning that the outfit, the hair, the nails, the makeup, the casket, all of that had to be perfect. If living had been hard, at least the exit would be a grand event.

Older black people made sure they had burial insurance if they didn't have anything else when they died. It was a reflection of how they had lived life in those days even if what they wanted never materialized. So, looking forward to Heaven and arriving in style was a sign to everyone that you had lived a life worthy enough to get rewards in heaven, to walk through the pearly gates. Those were the messages from church—repent so you can get into Heaven when God comes for you. Repent so that when this world ends, you will be worthy of being saved.

Helen's mother was well versed in this tradition, and she had burial insurance on her son, but she never thought she would have to use it so soon.

All Joe wanted was to get to know a pretty girl, and he received the ultimate punishment. Helen's thoughts couldn't stop vibrating in her body. She was numb when she sat in the church pew during the service. She was numb when she saw her family members carry out the casket covered in yellow roses out to the waiting limousine. She was numb sitting with her mother in the back of the family limousine as they drove to the cemetery for one more service.

She barely noticed the sun shining through the puffy clouds to bathe the mourners in a golden light. She had talked to a lot of her friends about death being a transition to a new beginning, but now that it was so personal, she was having a difficult time taking her own advice.

The Celebration of Life party was packed with family and friends and neighbors. Of course, they all had something kind to say about Joe to Helen to her face, but when her back was turned, she heard the accusatory comments about Joe's unfortunate choice of a girlfriend. She couldn't take it anymore.

She walked to the front of the room and tapped on a glass with a big spoon.

"I have something to say to those of you who think my brother Joe got what he deserved."

The room went silent.

"He was the best brother a girl could have. He protected me, he made me laugh and no one deserves to be murdered for wanting to walk down a street with a pretty girl." Tears were running down Helen's cheeks. "And so those of you who think he asked for this, I pray that you are not judged for trying to be happy in your life when someone disagrees with you."

Helen walked back to her mother, "Sorry mama. I had to say this."

"You are a brave and wonderful child," she said. "I am so proud of you, and you will be an inspiration to all in our family."

*   *   *

That night as Helen lay in bed trying to go to sleep, she thought about the day's events and how she ended it. Finally, turning over and dozing off she started to dream. She and Joe were in a canoe on a lake, paddling over to a small island in the middle. The air was filled with blackbirds and gold butterflies hovering over them in a cloud of fluttering color. She could feel the soft lapping of the water against the boat as a gentle vibration. She was filled with such joy, because she knew that she would always be able to find her brother in this life or the next anytime she wanted. He was waiting for her. Water was their shared experience, and, in that moment, she decided that the house she chose as her family house would be situated on a lake. It would be a big house, big enough for the extended family to come and visit, big enough for her to grow.

CHAPTER 4

The First House

Helen was walking along one of the old, battered streets in Ann Arbor, Michigan, on the way home from school. She was in her senior year and was a little lost in what she wanted to do after she graduated. It was February and still cold and blustery, and she was bundled up in her purple parka with a gold and black wool scarf wrapped around her neck. She looked over at one of the old houses that had seen better days and needed some love. There was a For Sale sign in the front yard. Even that was kind of battered.

She stopped and stared at the house and felt a sadness inside. At one time the house was full of people and life. There was a small rusty pail and shovel half hidden in the overgrown flower bed, a sure sign that children had lived here. She wondered about the meals they ate, the laughter shared, and a baby that might have been born and brought home to this house. And now the season had changed. Somehow all the life that was once here, was gone. But not quite. Something was beckoning her to come closer, so she walked up the sidewalk and looked in the dirty front window. It was kind of a mess, but the room looked like a nice size. It was the oddest feeling. She could almost see who had once lived here. Something inside her said *This can be reborn. This home can come back to life for another family.*

The sadness inside her fell away. The house started to glow. Not a big sunny glow, but a faint wispy glow that filled her with a quiet confidence that she may have discovered her next project. *I am going to buy you,* she thought. Without a doubt she knew she could clean up this house and make it presentable again. She knew how to polish floors and wash windows, and paint walls that needed a soft pale yellow to bring the sunshine back in. She could envision the whole process and spent the next half hour walking around and looking in all the windows. Nothing seemed too difficult.

"This house will make someone a great home," she whispered to herself, not a bit worried about finding the money. She just had to point someone in the right direction.

She wrote down the address and continued her walk to her family home.

"Hi Mom," she said. "Is there anybody in the family who lend me some money? I found a house I'm going to buy."

"Helen, what in the world are you talking about?"

"It's only three streets over from here and it needs some tender loving care, but I know I can make a lot of money on it. What do you think?"

Helen's mother, to her credit, did not laugh at her or tell her she was crazy. She had seen her daughter do a lot of things that no one expected.

"Show me the house and I will see if Uncle Julius is interested," she said.

The next morning Helen took her mother to look at the house. Her mother didn't even flinch at the peeling paint and broken sidewalk. She couldn't see what her daughter saw, a home that had possibilities with the right buyer, but she trusted her instincts.

Uncle Julius took a look and loaned Helen the purchase price, which was a bargain because of the time of year and the cosmetic updates desperately needed.

Helen spent the next three months cleaning up the place after school and on the weekends. In her mind she held a constant vision of the house, clean, lovely, and welcoming, and by the time Spring rolled into town, the front yard had tulips and daffodils, the house was freshly painted and the windows washed. She put a For Sale sign back into the yard with her mother's telephone number listed. That night, she received three calls, all wanting to see the house.

Helen's instincts had led her to that place. She was pulled to that place. She knew it. It was hard to explain that to anyone else. They all thought she just happened to be at the right place at the right time. That was okay. Only she knew the truth. She doubled Uncle Julius' money and became his partner. He was so impressed with her skills at seeing the value in old properties that he never questioned her. Just asked her how much. Soon she was all over town checking out old houses that just needed someone to notice them. Helen noticed.

It was that faint glow that she saw on each property that was the right one for her to invest in. She called it her spirit guide pointing out the properties that would benefit from her sense of when it was right to save lovely old homes that needed a new family.

Helen was responsible for a dozen families finding homes that were welcoming and fresh. And she gained a lot of new friends who were grateful for her discerning eyes.

CHAPTER 5

Meeting the Love of Her Life

On one of her jaunts around town looking at houses, Helen decided to take a break inside a small diner. When she walked past, she couldn't ignore the smell of fresh baked pumpkin pie wafting out the door. She started salivating and couldn't remember the last time she ate. When Helen got involved in a search, she could go the whole day without eating. Her mother scolded her every time, "Helen, you will waste away to nothing. You must feed yourself or you will get sick, and then who will find those homes for people desperate for new starts."

She wasn't quite sure how her daughter did what she did, but she could see that Helen was happy with her focus on this odd career when she was so young. And she was astounded at how smart Helen was when it came to her ability to keep on budget when renovating these houses. Her Uncle Julius, who was also smart at running a business was a perfect mentor to get her started and to help keep her motivated.

Helen walked into the diner and sat in a red leather booth by the window. It was in between the rush hour of breakfast and lunch so no problem taking up the whole booth. She laid out her notes from all the houses she'd seen that morning trying to decide which would be her next big find. Each house had merits, but only one glowed when she first looked at it. She should trust her instincts. She hadn't been led astray yet, but she was still a little nervous about spending that much money.

"What can I get you, hon?" The waitress laid a menu down in front of her.

Helen didn't even look. She already knew. "I smell pumpkin pie like it just came from the oven. I would like a slice and a coffee with two creams and one sugar." She handed the menu back to the waitress. "Thank you, Peggy," she said noticing the nametag pinned to her uniform's front pocket.

"Good choice. I had a small piece myself for breakfast before I started work. It's delicious." Peggy said as she turned back to the kitchen.

She returned a few minutes later and slid the plate with the pumpkin pie in front of Helen. Then she filled the coffee cup with steaming black coffee, placed a small pitcher of cream and a small bowl of sugar in the center of the table.

"Enjoy. Let me know if you need anything else."

"Thank you, I will." Helen took a bite of the pie and swooned. "Wow. This is amazing," she said softly.

The diner door opened and a young man, tall and very fit walked in and grabbed a stool at the counter. He ordered coffee and pumpkin pie. He too must have been captured by the fresh baked smell coming out the diner door. At first Helen didn't notice him. Then she stopped when she heard him talking to the waitress. The voice was deep and rich and almost musical. A tingle ran down her spine. She had never heard a voice quite like that before. She didn't want him to stop talking. She wanted to meet him, find out who he is, what he does and does he live in the neighborhood. Her mother would be shocked, but Helen got up from her seat in the booth and walked over to him, tapped him on the shoulder and said, "Excuse me. I saw you eating that amazing pumpkin pie. You look a little large for these counter stools. You could share my booth with me, if you want."

The young man looked up at her, a twinkle in his chestnut colored eyes. "Are you sure miss?" he asked, his voice rumbling like a purr.

Helen was smitten for the first time in her life. Her heart hammered as she met those warm, sparkling eyes. She managed a smile that felt both confident and shaky at the same time. "I'm sure. I mean, if you'd like the company. I'm Helen."

She gestured toward her booth by the window, suddenly hyperaware of every movement she made. *What am I doing?* her practical side whispered, but that voice—that incredible voice—had short-circuited her usual caution.

The young man slid off the stool with an easy grace that contradicted his size, picking up his plate and coffee mug. "Skip," he said, extending his free hand. His hand-shake was firm but gentle. "And thank you. These stools weren't exactly built for comfort."

As they settled into the booth across from each other, Helen noticed the way the late morning light caught the steam rising from their coffee cups. It was like an aura between them, a connection that made her want to stay here and listen to him for the rest of the day. Skip took a bite of his pie. "Oh dear Jesus, that is some delicious pie," he said.

Helen found herself strangely nervous, playing with her fork, almost afraid to look at him. She knew he was older than her, old enough that her mother would be really annoyed and her father downright awful. At that moment she wished her brother, Joe was still around. He had always protected her from her father's temper. But when she thought about it, she felt a calmness descend on her like a soft silken fabric that soothed her heart. "Thank you, Joe. I know you are with me," she whispered softly to herself.

"So," she starts, then laughs at herself. "I should prob-ably mention I don't usually do this. Walk up to strangers in diners, I mean."

Skip's smile was slow and genuinely amused. "Well, I'm glad you made an exception. This pie's good, but the company's better." He paused, studying her with open curiosity. "You from around here? I don't think I've seen you in the neighborhood before."

"I've been house hunting actually," Helen says, relaxing slightly. "Looking for properties that need some work. Fix them up, resell them. What about you? Do you live nearby?"

She realizes she's leaning forward, genuinely interested in whatever he's about to say. Her mother's imagined shock fades to nothing. This feels right somehow, spontaneous and terrifying but perfect.

They spent the next three hours talking, sharing stories. It was as if they had known each other in another life. She insisted on buying him lunch, which he found oddly endearing. Here was a young woman who was independent, very pretty and ambitious in a good way. And he was shocked to discover when she told him she was seventeen. He would have to be careful with this one. He was already falling in love with her. He loved that she was making homes for people.

He told her about his family. She was shocked to hear that he was the oldest of eighteen children.

"Wow, that's a lot of birthdays to remember and Christmas presents to buy. How do you do it?" Helen looked at Skip with her mouth open.

"First of all, I keep a calendar of events for my entire family. Otherwise, I would never be able to remember all of the birthdays and other celebrations. Second, I ask my mother. She knows everything. I find the women in my life are much better at keeping track of things in general. And to make it more interesting, I spent my childhood traveling the country as the child of a military man."

"Oh, your poor mother," said Helen. "Setting up house for that large a family each time you had to move."

"She was fierce, I must say that. Each time my father was redeployed, she would start searching for housing in the local papers of where we were going next. As a military family we received a lump sum of money, and of course, not all the kids were born yet. By the time mom and dad and created number eighteen he had been retired from the military for a couple of years."

"I have six brothers and sisters, and I know how chaotic even that can be. I can't imagine eighteen."

"We have a lot of bunkbeds in the bedrooms. The smallest ones sleep together. Once the kid reaches ten years old, they get their own bed."

"So, what do you do now? If you don't mind me asking." said Helen.

"I followed in my father's footsteps and joined the military. I just finished serving four years in the United States Army stationed throughout Germany."

"Wow, I haven't been anyplace yet, but I have always wanted to travel." Helen looked wistfully out the window. "There is so much to see that I have only read about."

"I love traveling. I really have the bug now. The military gave me that chance to experience a different part of the world after visiting every state in this country, except Alaska and Hawaii."

"What was your favorite place to visit," asked Helen, totally mesmerized by Skip's travel stories.

"I think I liked traveling by sea on the big ships the most. There was something enticing about the smell of the sea and the stars at night reflected on a dark ocean. Dolphins would sometimes follow the ships looking for handouts."

Helen looked ready to swoon listening to Skip's stories and now he had touched the thing that moved her the most. Traveling on water reminded her of her brother. She decided right then that Skip was going to be her forever love. *This is crazy, I just met him a couple of hours ago,* she thought.

Skip was also infatuated with this clever young woman who had already been successful in her life. He didn't want the day to end, but finally he said. "I could talk to you all day, but I have an appointment. I am now an electrician just getting started. Can't be late to my next job, though I am only giving them a quote. I know we have just met, but I would like to see you again, if you would like."

Helen blushed and shyly smiled. "I think I would like that, too. But you will have to pass my mother's inspection. She is very protective of me, and I am also protective of myself, if that makes sense."

"Sounds good. May I call on you tomorrow afternoon? Do you think your mother will be ok with that?"

"I will ask her, but she trusts my instincts on a lot of levels. Ever since my brother passed, I have to handle a lot of the responsibilities of the oldest child."

"I am sorry to hear about your brother . . ."

Helen looked down at her empty coffee cup. "I don't know why I even told you that. I hardly know you, but I feel like I have known you forever."

* * *

The next day Helen was so nervous she couldn't eat her breakfast.

"What's going on, baby girl?" Helen's mother asked as she watched her normally relaxed daughter twitching in her chair like a dog chasing a flea.

Helen took a deep breath. "I met someone yesterday and I said he could stop by to meet you. It was his idea; I swear to be so polite and ask your permission..."

"Hmmm. What's the catch? Why are you so fidgety?"

"Well . . . he's a little bit older than me. I met him at the diner, and we started talking and he was so interesting and polite and nice."

Helen's mother took a deep breath imagining the worst. "How much older?"

"Just 24. That's not too old. Wait 'til you meet him."

CHAPTER 6

Marriage and Careers

The meeting with Helen's mother went well. Skip impressed her with his good manners and respectful manner, and she recognized a man who knew that Helen wasn't ready yet. Skip took his time, realizing that Helen was still a girl and needed to grow into a woman before he asked her what he wanted to ask her almost as soon as he met her for the first time in that pumpkin pie smelling diner.

*   *   *

Helen got her bachelor's degree in finance which enabled her to establish her own CPA business. She was heads and tails above her classmates because of her experience negotiating loans for the properties she had already purchased.

Helen liked math and she was good at it. Math was certain. It didn't change. It was always predictable. Unlike life that ebbed and flowed, minute by minute, hour by hour, bringing in new paradigms and taking away others, math left nothing to mystery. That's why she picked accounting as her major. When she enrolled at the University of Michigan she excelled. All of the material she studied and learned was solid and sure. A method of structure she could count on in this ever-moving, ever-changing existence on earth.

Skip cheered her on in her studies, proud of her mastery of accounting. Accounting made her feel calm and in control despite her own chaotic family life.

Skip didn't sit on his laurels. While Helen was attaining her degree he went on to graduate from the Chrysler Training Center for Electrical Technicians as well as the Washtenaw Community College Culinary Arts Program. He loved to cook and was an excellent chef and could also fix all the electrical upgrades in Helen's housing business. Helen thought it was the perfect combination.

After a 3-year courtship, Skip Vining married Helen Epps of Monroe, Michigan, on March 21, 1977. To this union was born a son, Lamar Leon and a daughter Jasmine Allyn. Helen had no idea how much she would love being a mother, but little Lamar and Jasmine took her breath away. Skip was right there with her. He did not want a huge family. He was satisfied with these two little creatures who filled his days with love and laughter.

Both of their professional careers flourished, and their bank accounts grew. Helen knew how to invest because she understood all the machinations of compounded interest and stocks and bonds. She was saving for her children's futures.

Helen's accounting business, and her continued Real Estate investments continued to thrive, getting bigger and creating more prosperity for her and her family. Her instincts seemed infallible. When she looked at a property that others weren't always optimistic about, it was like she could see and feel its future potential.

People would scratch their heads when she would share her excitement about a property, "Helen, you sure about that? It doesn't seem like a very popular place to buy."

But when she knew, she knew. No one could dissuade her, and time and again they were shocked at the outcome when she achieved success after success. Her ability to do that allowed her to grow a healthy real estate portfolio and bless her family with everything they needed.

At the back of her mind her greatest driving force was her family and children. She had clear goals for them. She had decided she wanted to be worth millions so that when she passed, they would be taken care of in the style they were accustomed to. She had a vision and she had no doubt she would make her vision happen.

It was difficult not to spoil her beautiful children, but she knew they would have to find their own way to grow up to be strong and independent. She didn't talk about it to them. Better to surprise them when she was ready.

Helen was always in motion and at the same time, she kept her accounting business going. It was her bread and butter, and many people relied on her for financial advice. For Helen the accounting gave her a way to help bring financial stability to families. With proper accounting businesses would thrive, people wouldn't make tragic mistake that could devastate their future and their family. She loved being that stabilizing presence in the financial lives of her clients and friends, while earning a good income at the same time.

And she and Skip loved to travel. Their favorite trips involved cruising up and down rivers in the United States, then up and down the west coast to Alaska and down to the Mexican peninsula. Helen knew it was the affinity she had for water and how sacred it was to the planet and to life itself.

*   *   *

When Lamar Jr and Jasmine were old enough to stay with grandma for a couple of weeks, they decided to fly to Germany where Skip had been in the military to take a Viking River Cruise on the Danube. Winding through Germany, Austria, Hungary and five other countries, the Danube River was said to be the soul of Central and Eastern Europe. Scenic vineyards, captivating history and savory cuisine were more than they could have imagined. They strolled through Budapest's Castle District and across the famous Chain Bridge, enjoyed Vienna's renowned café culture reminiscing on how they had first met in a small diner with great coffee and pumpkin pie.

They attended a concert featuring works by Wolfgang Amadeus Mozart and Johann Strauss.

The journey on the "Blue Danube" was a captivating and unforgettable experience.

When they arrived back home, Helen went house hunting for her own family. She found a large house situated on a lake just outside Ann Arbor, Michigan. It had enough bedrooms to accommodate quite a few of their combined large families for holidays. And it had a large master bedroom overlooking the lake and away from all the racket of family and guests. It was hers and Skip's true sanctuary.

Aunt Helen's house, as it was called, became the favorite destination for their huge extended family.

CHAPTER 7

The Children in Her Life

Cousin Wendy stopped by to help Helen celebrate. It was Helen's granddaughter Miyana's Sweet Sixteen party. The house and backyard were decorated beautifully like a winter wonderland, even though it was the middle of summer. There were silver tinsel and white ribbons draped on the back porch. Silver stars were strung through the porch railings. The cake was three layers high with white frosting and silver fairies as candle holders. Lots of hustle dancing and good music, family and friends. Miyana was an only child and her parents adored her. She was a math prodigy and was still young, but so smart that colleges were already reaching out to her with scholarship offers. And yet she was still a little girl. She was dancing the hustle with a whole bunch of kids in a circle. They were laughing and teasing each other like children do. She was sixteen going on twelve at times and Helen adored her.

Helen had made sure that whatever happened, she would make sure that Miyana's tuition would be taken care of.

"Hard to believe, Helen that this precious little girl is now sixteen," said Wendy. "Pretty soon she will be going to the Senior Prom."

Hellen chortled, "I was asked to go to the Senior Prom by Mike Henderson and I said no. My mom was so mad, but what she didn't understand was that I was very depressed and overwhelmed at the time. There was so much going on, and I was expected to step up and be the adult. It was exhausting and I was not ready."

"WOW! Where in the world was Wendy," Wendy laughed. "But honestly, she was probably relieved. So much stuff happens during these Senior Prom parties, it would make your head turn."

"You got that right, my friend. I am so grateful that you are here with me and have talked me through some pretty dark moments. I know this all too well that my main sin is WORRY. I am better but I still need to work on it every day. Otherwise, it will rob me of the present and peace in my complicated life. It's what I must constantly acknowledge. I know that I am protected as a sovereign being, but I'm trying to keep my thoughts on faith strong and believe it's all good as well."

"It is human nature to be doubtful in this world," said Wendy. "But you have had prayers answered, and I know you don't believe in coincidence."

"I see more of divinity in certain situations. But still I struggle. I've had several supernatural events that have proven to me that there is spiritual energy that is forever in existence for anyone who reaches out. It's the weight lifting of prayer that we need all day, every day. I must remember when I'm getting extremely anxious, I'm using the wrong muscles. Fear instead of Faith."

"Well put, my friend. I will remember that. Turn it around, Faith instead of Fear," said Wendy.

"Skip always pointed out to our daughter Jasmine that God's glory is in the moon, the sun, the stars, and everything around it in nature. He is such a wonderful father. I think he is relieved, though, that we decided to limit our offspring to two children instead of the dozen his siblings kept teasing him about. Could you ever imagine? That would put me in an early grave if I had to deal with that many children on top of all of the dramas I detox in both of our families."

"I hear you, dear friend. I am so glad you are my cousin. On top of everyone else, you keep me grounded." Wendy took a sip of her non-alcoholic punch.

"Whenever the moon had different shapes, Jasmine would always take pictures and I would post them. Fast forward to today. People are looking at more and more posts and commenting on everything. I think it's great to get them to pay attention.

"One day about two years ago I talked to Jasmine about it, and she said people just don't pay attention to what is right in front of their eyes.

Wendy chuckled. "Like mother, like daughter."

"It is when we started visiting places where the water is so beautiful and the waves so strong, that I really started thinking about creation. It's beautiful and we have the senses to be awed by it. But we have to take time and be present in the moment, or it will pass us by.

"I kept sharing all of mine and Jasmine's beautiful photos and soon people started acknowledging them. I swear, more folks on my page post beautiful pictures of nature that they have taken the time to be aware of."

"Wendy patted her on the back, "It's because you brought it to their attention."

"Skip said that when he was distraught at seven years old leaving Michigan for Macon, Georgia — a culture shock, his stepmother talked to him about God. She then showed him a four o'clock flower and spoke about the greatness of God in nature's creations. He said when the flower opened, that convinced him and he started talking to God himself."

"Grandma, come and dance with us," laughed Miyana as she tugged at Helen's hand.

*   *   *

Helen's heart was deeply rooted in her love for family. As a dedicated mother and grandmother, she was the cornerstone of her family. Her grandchildren were her pride and joy, and she showered them with love, and endless support. Known as the family's genealogist, she meticulously documented their history and stories, ensuring that the legacy of her family's past would be preserved for generations to come. Skip was also involved in the life courses of his children and grandchildren and nieces and nephews. He took it as a responsibility to keep them on the right path and make sure their futures were set. He was the perfect partner for Helen and she never forgot it.

Helen was also a secret fairy godmother to other children who were struggling with poor family situations and poverty. She was generous with her help, both psychological and financial. She couldn't take care of everybody, and she had to weed out those people who were trying to use her for their own sake and not their children. Those stories made her angry. Skip helped her weed out the con artists. He was a force not to be reckoned with. One look at his imposing frame, his fierce eyes and his thundering voice usually took care of those people who dared to take advantage of his Helen.

CHAPTER 8

Deaths in the Family

It was a rainy fall day, and Skip and Helen were taking a little time together. Their huge families kept them always on the go, or sorting out messes, or helping with emergencies. They had both been busy with their various endeavors. Skip, as a master electrician and had just finished up a large project outside of Ann Arbor, working on a factory warehouse. Helen was always busy with her CPA business. Many of her clients from the local community valued her integrity and commitment to their financial well-being, as much as they did her friendship.

Skip knew about Helen's abilities to talk people through some of the worst moments in their life, when a family member was on their deathbed or had passed unexpectedly. He didn't know how she did it, but they talked about it a lot, because it seemed to take a lot out of her. He was always there for her, and would hold her tight when she couldn't keep the tears away even though she believed this was meant to be, that the people had passed their test to move onto another, brighter future.

Helen was the stalwart of the family. She was the foundation upon which so many family members relied. Skip understood the burdens she carried in that role and knew that to help sustain her, he needed to be the bedrock to support her. He remembered her talking about Aunt Priscilla's 90th birthday party. She had lost three children, her husband and some siblings and she just kept on going through each day, even with all of that sorrow. But Helen had been there for her. She was always there when needed.

Helen's Aunt Ruby died from a heart attack. She never recovered from Aunt Eunice's death when she got the news from her husband. She took to her bed on March 20,1990. That was devastating for Helen. She thought about how happy Aunt Ruby was for almost an entire year, getting her some medical attention to get better. The last thing she said was, "Helen thought I would be ok," but that wasn't the outcome. Aunt Ruby tried to get Helen and her father to come to her house at the same time to give them paperwork. Helen knew that she was planning to leave, and she wouldn't go to her house because she didn't want her to leave. She just couldn't go and cosign any papers with her. Aunt Ruby died February 26, 1991.

All of these deaths followed other deaths. Cousin Rock lost his sister, Mozell, the one he had cared for in Detroit most of his life and then his mother left followed by a nephew. Helen's grandfather left February 13, 1985.

By then she had buried two sisters and two brothers and both parents.

She had an inkling about Rock who had been very ill the year before. Skip had to fly back on short notice to say what would be the last goodbye.

Helen remembered buying those airline tickets and how happy Rock looked to see them that Thanksgiving. They were going to visit him again in December but that was not to be. He made his transition to the other side shortly after their Thanksgiving visit.

Skip lost his main parent, and Helen lost her mom, her emotional support. Those were the deaths that changed their entire existence as a couple, as parents.

Then, Skip's father left on February 5,1991.

* * *

Death ushers in a lot of separations, it reveals some folks' intentions in a way that only death can which is why fights are going to happen. There are the greedy, the needy, the guilty and all this pain lands with no cure. It starts attacks among families. Helen had been on this end far too many times. She was a mirror for people who show themselves thinking it won't be addressed and feel safe to come to her even knowing that she lost her husband and her baby sister.

The hardest deaths are the ones when a person is dying slowly, and everyone is hoping for a miracle. Those around them end up staying in a place called anticipatory grief, where they want to hang on to the person preparing for a promotion from this existence to the next, but they are still holding on for their loved ones. The only way to survive this is to realize that they are suffering and ready to move on, they need to move on.

The most blindsiding are the deaths that seemingly happen so unexpectedly that everyone is literally in shock. The mind has a hard time accepting that someone who you just interacted with as far as a week, the same day or the same hour is gone. This person appeared healthy, happy, just loving life with all its challenges. They were, it seemed, present for the continuation of their life. It is like Jane Doe is dead, and the response, "I just talked to her this morning you must be talking about someone else."

Then the calls start, people drop by, and after Skip's death Helen would have to pretend that she was there, but she was not. She couldn't be. Even those who cry, or collapse, even may require a hospitalization to recover from the shock, can never take in the totality of that change so there is a period of self-protection that keeps them standing.

Helen's Journal

The journey from birth to death is now known as the dash. It is what happens on the journey and will there be a sense of the difference in people's lives. Are there people willing to speak about who you were to them? What was your main trait that all can agree on? Were you caring, family oriented, God fearing, all good or were you a troublemaker, or whatever might be perceived as the main thing people saw in you. Was your energy light-filled, sad and broken, or just angry and dangerous?

* * *

Helen had heard words spoken or seen events unfolding that indicated that an exit was imminent. The soul was weary, and the spirit wanted out. She watched her dad who always joked that he wanted to make Methuselah look like a teenager. "He was the longest living person according to the Bible," he said to her. "You know, eventually this cancer gets you no matter what you do," when less than a year before he was in the fight for his own Methuselah years. After he said that, he died within six months. Helen's mother whose main goal in life was to outlive him started telling the caregivers that she would be going home to the Lord soon and to be with her husband. But she never discussed this with Helen. Her sometimes dementia made it too difficult. She left seven months later.

Helen's brother Cleve had apologized to her and Skip. He was waking up from a state of being where he had not been present for them. He was not happy with how he had handled a lot of things.

Helen's brother Marvin had been a healer, but he was not able to heal himself, but he told her, "Whether we know it or not, some of us can feel how long we will be here especially those whose time is short. We try to live every day to the fullest. Sometimes it's hard, sometimes it's full of light and love, like leaving fresh scents behind wherever we go."

Marvin had heard Helen and adopted her mental strength to deal with his own death. She was grateful that she had made a difference in his life at the end.

Helen's Journal - on Death

Some people are promoted to the next plain even though they cannot do what has given them the most purpose. If you are giving people life through art all your life and then you can't do it any more, then you are done. When you are a person who brings laughs and joy to others but now are just giving off feel-sorry vibes, you are done. When you are a nurturer and have no one left to nurture you are done. When you are a protector, a leader, one who handles all the challenges and can no longer handle these challenges because you are trapped in a body that doesn't reflect your spirit anymore, you are done.

When your tribe has started to ascend maybe all at once maybe over a short period of time, the struggle to stay is real. The folks that make it into their 80s, 90s even into the hundreds, have a sense of faith in God, in life and themselves.

To live amongst chaos, pain, struggle, and hate and keep waking up every morning is fascinating especially when there isn't money to allow for many comforts and adventures. These are the kind of people who are extremely grateful for every-thing—for the ground, the bird, the flower—but their belief in God being in charge stands out. Their stories could be full of pain, but they have overcome hardships that make them so resilient that life's unforeseen occurrences don't shake them. When they say the good die young, I can understand that. If you are awake and see so much unnecessary pain and you can't handle it, you can't stay here anymore. Every horrible act, every injustice, the hate, the jealousy, the greed, the lies, the quest for power instead of peace, lust instead of love, differences instead of commonality, all the things that separate us are upfront. Why stay for this?

The biggest group of humans who are not struggling for basics are in denial about life when it comes to death. The only way to live it is to act as though you will never die, never leave here for another location. It is mostly never a predicted date when you enter as to when you will leave, so that is the way we go about life, with all the deaths that have hit so many since the pandemic has exposed everyone to loss. At this point in my journey, I really want to celebrate all of these people leaving and how they lived."

Death is the only thing in life that is fair. We will all experience it. Death stays around me because without it my life would have never been lived fully. In a funny way, I was exposed to it at birth.

* * *

Helen was named after her aunt who died. She saw the first body of a person she admired when she was perhaps five and immediately knew that whatever remains she saw, she was still looking for the essence of him. She would've had a sister, but she also died right before Helen turned five. The thing that she wanted most in a house full of males was a sister, so there it was.

The news was filled with death. There were stories about the shootings of innocents that filled her with fear about death. As she sat next to her father, she watched the JFK funeral, and the shooting of Lee Harvey Oswald and Jack Ruby play out over and over on the tv. Then her grandmother died, and she saw what it was like for her father and his siblings. Shortly thereafter her father died. It was a complete game changer. His exit would dictate how Helen lived most of her life. His death was so very difficult but in looking back, and she said with complete conviction, "It was the biggest gift I could receive."

His death made her realize how precious family was—how important it is to get in as many memories, to be careful how you interact with them whenever you are around them because it could be last time you ever saw them.

It also made her aware of her own mortality. Helen was scared to death or maybe scared to life but within all these losses is the key to really living with intention. She had to experience death to get that moment to reflect on *why I am here why are we all here and what is this life all about.*

* * *

Helen's Journal - More on Death

Does my life mean anything to anyone else and did I use my time wisely? Do I spend time with loved ones making memories? Do I live in the present? Am I spiritually in-tune? Is my life authentic and, what does that mean? Quantity over quality seems to be the goal for most of us while some only care about their own experiences. If you are filled with happiness and accomplishing goals and feel good and surrounded in love and can do whatever, whenever, you will want the ride to last forever. And whenever you leave your name will be recognized—well known, hopefully for making a difference in some positive way.

Today when I hear of someone's death, I want to clap for them, not their family but for them for graduating, for completing this assignment and for a gathering of people who know you well enough to celebrate your journey, to comfort your loved ones and to hopefully let them feel joy at how you impacted others. I forgave quicker with loved ones because I knew that any moment they could be promoted, this would incite others to cross boundaries, but for rhetorical purposes. For the most part, I was at least a B grade in achieving this. I make lots of memories, say I love you often, break bread with loved ones, try to be kind and most of all live like I might not be here tomorrow, in this form anyways.

I believe we create our eternity with how we live in human form. If your world was always dark, sad, dangerous even, with your own free-will, you will probably come back because you can age out of the dark and try again. But perhaps it's different when your exit has everything to do with you not being able to handle the coldness of this dimension now or never again. Maybe they needed only a short time here before their journey in human form was finished.

Lately, the celebrations have been some of the kindest, happy, living life with joy moments, that when they enter or leave a room, their absence is felt.

* * *

Helen watched when her grandkids don't react to hearing of a transition. So many people close to them have left. Suicides and homicides have been a fact of life for many young people these days. She thought some of them don't fear death as a finality. She knew that indeed the end of this life isn't the finale, but not in the way it works playing video games. These games are violent and characters are eliminated, but in kids' minds, it is only a game. Her concern was the games shaped the kid's conscience with a kind of callousness about life and death.

Helen's Journal – How We Die

Major events that kill many like hurricanes, earthquakes, fires, natural disasters, and some man-made as well. Ships, cars, planes, medicines, and wars all seem unfair as these events often seem like preventable, accidents. I would venture to say there aren't any such things as accidents or coincidences, but there is fate, there is destiny, there is completion, and sometimes death can give life to a new way to exist on this dimension. The small-ness—the vulnerability of everyone—is on full display and they must think higher or perhaps lower in anger or revenge mode, but character is always revealed in the loss. The hardest part about transitions is when they occur in family groups, like one spouse of many years dies, a great percentage of the time the other spouse won't live too much longer. A parent los-ing a child puts the parents well as the children's siblings at risk. The parent the children, grandparents and grandchildren, best friends can be hit hard because it seems persistent after so many sympathy cards. Enough already. The living must move forward and go on living. Time is precious.

*   *   *

At some point Helen lost phone contacts, phone num-bers for everyone—all relatives and friends and business acquaintances. She wasn't sure if she didn't do it on pur-pose just to give herself a break. She had lost so many relatives and friends she thought people would be afraid to be around her. Like those who were might be thinking they were the next in line if they were still standing. But so much loss created an evolution in Helen's spirit that she believed happens to people who have been forced to endure a lot of loss. You evolve to a place where you begin to a feel at times there's nothing left to lose, so nothing to fear and no fear of death is quite freeing.

Her cousin Wendy was an exception to the rule. She always seemed to be available to talk to and for Helen to share more thoughts about this earthly plane, living and dying than she could ever write down.

Wendy was sitting on the porch with Helen after a particularly difficult day talking to some friends about accepting death as a requirement for living.

"For most of us," Helen said. "I think it has always been the fear that you never know when or how it will happen—besides terminal illnesses or accidents that leave you sick for a while, but that unknowingness is the same for most everything in life. We like to prepare for the next second, the next minute. We schedule activities throughout our day. We wake up with intentions that at a certain point, something is expected to take place."

"Amen to that," said Wendy. "It is so difficult to have plans go astray, just when you think you have it all figured out. I expect this to happen because I did this . . ."

"Sure, expectations are necessary for something to motivate us outside of just sitting with ourselves. I'm making a list that will include all the ones I have experienced and how they affected my movement on this journey to just accepting it all even when I am shaken and knocked down. We need lessons in how to prepare for the lost anger finding its way into our souls when people don't die according to our plan. You can't tell people how you feel when they have passed on. How dare they." Helen and Wendy both chuckled at that.

"This part dims the light of celebration because it is a hope that in honor of the person you honor him unconditionally. It is not about the mourners; it is about their promotion to the next level. The respect that is due is paid not to heal your void, your guilt, your anger, your pain, it is to honor and celebrate this one time in space the person who left us. What you gained from the experience of knowing them is how you make friends with death. You recognize the beauty of the soul's spirit as best you can."

"Wow," said Wendy. "And this time I am not referring to Where in the World is Wendy. Ha!"

"A soul's promotion is not the time for you to go and attack others for whatever you are feeling. When we realize that this is not the time to start regretting our interactions with a person, all our negative thoughts about how others become the focus instead of the person and how they handled the journey. Nothing else is important. Except maybe another cup of tea and some rhubarb pie?"

"You got me there darlin', bring it on."

After taking a much needed coffee and pie break Helen and Wendy sat for a while longer, letting the warm fall evening breezes fill them with the beauty of trees still green and the yellow blooms of Sneezeweed, deep purple of Ironweed and the glorious Joe-Pye Weed with tall pink and purple blossoms, a favorite of butterflies.

"Graveyards can be very peaceful. I and my friends hung out in graveyards as a good place to skip school. I never felt that sitting amongst the gravestones was anything other than peaceful. I just knew those peoples' spirits were around their designated spot in that place. So, I would think from that energy there is peace in death—for that soul to shed that human container and become one who is free of separateness, hate, jealousy and sickness and at one with all or God."

"How does Skip handle this burden you have to bear? It must weigh heavily on him also," asked Wendy.

"You know Skip," said Helen. "He is my rock, my support, my everything. He doesn't let people get so close that they crowd me, if he can help it. And he is an awful good cook. He made this rhubarb pie. What do you think?"

Wendy took another bite. "How did you find this treasure? You said you met him in a diner?"

"Yup. And he met my mother the next day and won her over with his gracious, sexy self."

Wendy went quiet, then said. "Do you remember my friend who passed last year from a heroin overdose? I knew something was wrong, but I always felt like I didn't try hard enough to get her help. I still blame myself even though inside I knew that there was nothing I could do. She had to decide herself to let this lethal addiction go. No one could talk her out of it. I still don't know what pain she was hiding."

"The only peace you have from something like this is knowing that you cared enough to try, and I am sure, deep down, she knew that too."

They both sat quietly for a few moments remembering those who chose to leave. Helen believed that no one left before their time. Their time was just on a different clock that didn't correlate with everybody else's watch.

Helen knew from a young age that death has its own meaning with each person.

Deaths from old age, accidents, or health issues all carry their own signature of grief. The period of mourning for each person will be different in these instances. The patriarch death can lead to so many losses or is preceded by loss of one close to them. Losing loved ones can sometimes lead to group loses. Those connections at birth are just as powerful as those in death.

The free spirit, of course, stays here for a much shorter time. They can't stand the confinement. However, they often leave their mark. In the short time they are here, life in its totality as it is seen and heard by them in a unique and sometimes rebellious way. Oftentimes they are rejected for not conforming. Tired of the hate, their souls just want to go. Unexpected, quick, seemingly out of nowhere deaths fit that category.

Those suffering illnesses or emotional pain unresolved leading to addictions that can accelerate their departure from this earth, but still their suffering usually happens over a prolonged period of time.

"Everyone will die and most of the time we have not been trained to think that we could expect it other than knowing a body is deteriorating. It can be detected by paying attention to those around us and their attitude during their journey. There are words spoken that could indicate they were ready, or they knew. I believe so from the ones I have been close to, and it has always been something that grabbed me as a little girl. I can talk about its impact on me and my faith and in my love of people. Watching it should not be feared but celebrated. Death should stop being a curse word, or a fear of the unknown. Unexpected timing is normal when it comes to death. There is death by illness, death by age, death by someone else's hands, death by surprise, death by negligence, death by weariness, and death's embrace of a loved one."

Helen's Journal - Our Tribe

When we are born into a group—a tribe—in this life, that will form our perceptions. This is experienced by many of us when we enter this world. With the same DNA and history, we share a journey with them. First, our birth order, our time of entry. Our parents' assignments greatly influence our moves out the gate. There is a different route for those enjoying their time here. The ones at the top of the food chain tend to be the ones with the most knowledge, resources, lineage, talents and gifts. Their purpose is always obvious through their wealth and positions and just sometimes knowing their own destiny and responsibility. Sometimes expectations one feels are great from the world's perception or knowing in your spirit, that you have a great and challenging assignment to fulfill.

*   *   *

Helen remembered reading that Martin Luther King had tried to commit suicide more than once in his childhood. She felt this deeply and perceived that he understood the pain and injustices of this country, of this world, and that knowledge and knowing in his spirit overwhelmed him to the point of not wanting to go on. It was his destiny to change the narrative; to go down a road he hadn't prepared for. Fortunately, after some rough early year experiences, he was ready when it was presented. She felt the burden of the realization that his family had to live with the fear of knowing that he probably wouldn't grow to be elderly. He had shown that fear upon hearing what he perceived as gunshots. He flinched, he ducked, he was prepared for bullets to strike him. He spent some years out in the field with death threats and fires and jail and away from his wife and his children. They would come to know him more from the world's perspective of his fight for civil rights than the time he sacrificed away from his family and his children who would grow up without him. Helen registered the weight of the speech was played over and over indicating that he felt that death was near. She could feel he was tired of the burden of trying to win not just rights, but to change hearts. His journey in this country was almost a guarantee of an early transition and to become a hero whose mission would not be understood until decades later—planting seeds but not seeing the tree grow.

Helen's Journal –
Malcom X and Martin Luther King

Malcolm and Martin both died at thirty-nine leaving behind young wives and children, whose lives were safe to celebrate once years had passed. Their words were often quoted even though they both left here in violent ways. It can be and is oftentimes lost that their time here is not celebrated as much as we focus on the assassinations, as if that ended the goal, that the mission hadn't been accomplished. Murder always seems to stop an expected outcome, robbed us of them. The entire world lost a chance to rise up so we mourn that person so much harder, not with anger or resentment, but regret for what was, what could have been, and a sense of doom from their departure. So, the mourning time for everyone will be different in the instances of accidents where unexpected, quick, nowhere deaths take us by surprise. In this case we don't have a chance to say goodbye or correct that last hurtful thing we may have said to them. That causes a lot of self-doubt saying, if only I had done this, if only I had said that. Illnesses or addictions that lead to death leave people emotionally drained because they spent so much time trying to make it better. Losing loved ones can sometimes lead to a shared group loss, when nothing the family did could make any difference."

CHAPTER 9

Losing the Love of Her Life

Helen was talking to her Aunt Jeanine who asked her about premonitions, "One day I saw a casket floating in the air. Then it settled down to the ground and I heard weeping, but there was no one in the casket. The casket was transparent, so I knew it was a vision of something that had just happened or would happen soon. Then the next day I found out that my therapist's 37 year old son had been shot and killed. She never told me. She said she couldn't talk about it for the longest time, but now she accepted it. The whole thing gave me chills.

She told me that after hearing testimony that he left the scene that was starting to become dangerous but then he choose to return. She realized that God had given him a chance to walk away from an escalating situation, but he made the choice to intervene, that it was his choice. She was better able to accept that he followed his own will to try and make a difference, but he sacrificed his own life to do so.

"I believed we know what's right and can decide even when others don't. It hadn't been a year since her son's passing but she had made peace. I know she is really walking in faith. It makes you aware of God's presence because, initially, after a loss you need to be carried by God's spirit to a place where you can accept what has happened. It was obvious once I spoke with her that she's under God's umbrella right now.

Helen paused and looked at her aunt. "And it's always been my feeling that I know for sure the people that I am going to lose. Most of them also knew their time to transition was drawing near. But there was a sense of them completing their mission to me. And I was able to guide them through the portal of a new beginning. Once they realized that they would connect with their loved ones who have already transitioned, they would relax and accept the coming journey without fear."

Helen's experience with death made her realize not to ever take life for granted. Dealing with her own sickle cell illness made her more aware than a lot of folks about the precious moments of life. She thought that people don't have the right perspective on death. She continued, "I know the life we live on this mortal plane is just a temporary state, but most people try to do as much here as possible, as if they going to stay here forever.

"People almost never ask, "Why am I here?" Because they're so distracted by what this world offers. I think the young people are more aware of the possibilities in this world as well as the next because they're not as engrossed in programming as we were when we were young.

Her aunt reached out and touched her arm, "Oh Helen, you have always been connected to the power and energy in this life form we inhabit, but you never seemed to be afraid of death. I wish I could feel that way."

Helen thought about what she said. "I think that I've lived a better life, and I've had more supernatural connections, because I've always had it in my mind that I was going to leave here. Knowing this is a tragedy and a gift, caused me to believe I could never take anything for granted. So, I started out writing letters to each family member, letting them know how I felt about this life and offering them the chance to share their fears and expectation.

"When our close friends and family die, we're not just sad, which we should be because we're not going to see them anymore. We start wailing, "oh, they die too soon.

"And I like the word *pass* when people die. *That person passed*. I think that actually is a pass to a promotion to the next level that God has planned for us. So, my intention is to make people more aware that this is a temporary journey, and we have things to do here, to help each other and not to be afraid of that, but to embrace it.

"But if somebody came and asked me, "If you could have them back, would you say yes?" I would say, "Oh, no, they did what they were supposed to do. Why would I have them come back here if they already passed their test? Even if I miss them terribly. It's not my right to change their journey only because I feel guilty about things I did or said and would like another chance at rewriting the personal history book of our relationship.

"And each death makes one remember the arguments and the guilt. I cried yesterday when I thought about my husband, but that's just a new way of living."

Helen stopped and stared at the sky for a couple of minutes, totally lost in her memories of her beloved Skip. Then she continued. "The whole family was in shock when Skip transitioned because it happened while we were on a world cruise that had stopped in Sicily. We were going to stay in this gorgeous little hotel overlooking the sea for a couple of days while the cruise ship refitted its supplies. So far, the cruise had been glorious, traveling across all that water made me feel like I was in constant contact with my brother. It was almost as if I could see him floating in the waves and smiling that sweet, gentle smile. Of course, he still looked 18 years old, and I wondered if he recognized his sister who was now in her sixties.

"The Pandemic had caused all the concierge service people to be forced to stay at home and Skip had to lift all our luggage to put it in the taxi. All of a sudden, he grabbed his chest and called my name. Then he dropped to the ground right in front of me. I must admit, I didn't see that one coming exactly like that. I knew he wasn't feeling well but I thought we would have more time, a lot more time. He was so strong looking and still movie-star handsome. I screamed for help, but most of the trauma services were overloaded with Covid emergencies and it took a while before a small, battered ambulance arrived. I was holding his hand, begging him not to leave me when the medical technicians gently pulled me away and loaded him into the ambulance. I insisted and got into the back of the vehicle with him. I didn't speak much Italian, only a couple of words but I made them understand that I was going with him, no matter what. I sat there holding his hand knowing that his transition had been quick, so he didn't suffer. But I was so upset and angry at first. How could he ever leave me? We were perfect together, did everything together and he was irreplaceable.

"When we arrived at the hospital, it was chaos. People were everywhere, crying for their family members who hadn't made it through the pandemic, and they had no place to put all the bodies. I knew Skip was gone but I was not going to leave him alone."

"But this was finally the most unbearable death of all to me. My beloved soul mate, the rock of my life, the one who understood and adored me left the earth suddenly and unexpectedly. Elmer "Skip" Leon Vining III, age 69, transitioned on January 28, 2020, in Sicily, while he was traveling on a world cruise, doing what he loved best with me. We were living our best life." Helen paused and wiped the tears streaming down her cheeks.

"So what did you do?" Jeanine asked. "I can't imagine how frightening that must have been for you, in a foreign country during a world pandemic crisis."

Helen answered, a faraway look in her eyes, "I had just lost the love of my life, but I realized that he had transitioned and he would always be with me, no matter what. That gave me a strength that I didn't know I had. He had always been my rock, my lifeline to protect me from those who tried to drag me down. And now I had to be strong enough to get him back home to his family."

"When I think about it, I remember when the car drove up to the hospital, a rainbow appeared right in front of me. I started having all these supernatural occurrences. Because once something like that happens to you never the same, right? That got me home from Sicily. I was still trying to figure out what happened to me all the way around.

"If you have self-awareness, and self-realization born out of trauma, you become who you are."

Helen told Jeanine that the first thing she had to do was contact the US Embassy/Consulate. They told her she had to hire a local funeral home to prepare the remains (embalming, sealed casket) and handle local requirements Then she had to get a death certificate, a Consular Report of Death Abroad (CRODA): Prepared by the U.S. embassy, useful for U.S. legal matters; CDC/Customs Documents: The body needs a death certificate (or consular mortuary certificate if unavailable) and a permit for importation, showing the cause of death and compliance with CDC rules for human remains. Increased focus on communicable diseases meant strict adherence to CDC rules for embalming and container sealing, even for non-communicable deaths like heart attacks, to avoid holding remains at U.S. ports.

The list of things she had to do was almost insurmountable so she did the only thing she could think of. Because Skip had been in the Army, she contacted the American Command Post in Sicily, and they agreed to expedite his removal back to the states, including flying his casket home on a military transport. She contacted The Merkle funeral home in Ann Arbor, Michigan, to receive his remains.

The Army helped her through all the paperwork. They were well versed in the requirements for returning a U.S. citizen home. Helen was exhausted and forever grateful for the help she received so far away from home. Her around-the-world vacation ended with a punch in the stomach, and she wasn't sure how she was going to pick up the pieces of her life.

But this was Helen, of course she did.

Like she had told her therapist, Jeannine. "I've lost all these people, especially my husband, which changed my life completely. But I have never felt that he left me on purpose.

The funeral was odd. Because of the Covid restrictions, they were only allowed to have a parking lot service, with no one getting out of their cars to hug each other in their grief. Skip never liked to be fussed over, so Helen thought he would be ok with this adjustment to the normal funeral ritual. One of his sisters got out and stood on the back of a red pickup truck with a speaker and microphone and sang a beautiful version of Amazing Grace. Helen and Skip's son, Lamar brought out his iPhone and put it next to the microphone. "Since my dad loved Jimmi Hendrix, I thought I would play his favorite "electric church" song. He pushed the button and wringing tones of Jimmi's guitar filled the whole neighborhood with "All Along the Watchtower" exploring salvation, prayer, and the search for peace, incorporating gospel-like calls and spiritual yearning for a better world.

Everyone was crying and honking their horns at the end of the service. It was a perfect finish and a new beginning for everyone there,

The Miracle

Then Helen's grandson came to visit her. She had to tell him that Poppy had passed. He was nine going on ten, and he started crying. He said, "Poppy is always with you. You just don't believe it. Like he's always there, and he says, you have a spirit height, and you have a guardian angel."

He told Helen the angel was pure light, and he's always around her. He was crying, and he was telling his grandma all this stuff, and then she thought to herself, *are you channeling something, or you just have been given these messages to give to me?* And he described the situation so vividly and truthfully, it felt like he was feeling everything.

When Helen told her cousin this story, he looked at her, a strange gleam in his eye. "Helen, watch for a miracle. It will prove to you that you are right about everything you believe about the next portal we travel through when we are ready. And the protections we received from our Guardians when it is not our time."

Two weeks later two teenagers were trying to blow up a school in Cokeville, Wyoming. They had 136 kids and 18 adults trapped in the building. The boy had rigged up the building with a bomb so it would blow up when they pulled the switch. They were asking for $2 million per child.

When the bomb was triggered, the only person who died was the girl who was holding the switch, and it accidentally went off. It was a miracle that no other lives were lost, though some were injured. And it was weird, because all these bomb experts were trying to explain how it didn't make sense, that the way it was set, it should have blown everyone to pieces. But instead, it just went straight up into the air.

Afterwards, children and teachers reported seeing figures they described as angels, deceased relatives, or bright lights who instructed them to go to a specific window, told them everything would be all right, and formed a protective ring around the bomb.

Later, when Helen told her cousin what happened, that it was the miracle he foretold, he started crying. She knew he was telling her the truth but just watching him and not knowing where it's coming from, it felt truly supernatural.

CHAPTER 10

Cruising with Cousin Wendy

It was 2022 and most of the Covid restrictions had calmed down. Helen was functioning as best she could without her beloved Skip. Every once in a while, she would smell his cologne in the bedroom or hear a faraway whisper of his deep baritone voice that always sent shivers through her body down to her toes. *No man should have a voice that sexy. It's no wonder I fell in love with him the minute he opened his mouth,* she thought.

In the meantime, she had a whole brood of nieces and nephews and grandchildren to entertain with her funny stories. One of her main themes was accountability, so she wove that into the stories. The little kids favorite was about *The Responsible Rabbit,* who learned how to take care of his things and how to be a good friend. There were other stories that taught lessons about respect and never giving up. Helen enjoyed them as much, if not more than the children who gathered around her. She always felt hope bloom in her heart when she saw the shining eyes looking up at her.

"Don't look to me. You need to talk to God, because he is your source, not me. Ta Da!" she laughed.

*   *   *

The one thing that was a weight on her mind, was the book she had been working on. It was an overwhelming project that she needed help on, so she reached out to her publisher. He agreed they could finish it for her if she gave them her main points to include. Helen was a talker and spent hours sharing her philosophies in life. She was sure that her book was in good hands.

*   *   *

Helen had retired to her oversized, lonely bedroom to try to grab a quick cat nap. There were a lot of people coming over for dinner. *Too many people, I don't think I can handle any more people telling me how sorry they are*, she thought.

"Helen, are you there?" called out Cousin Wendy in her upbeat perky voice. "I've got a great idea, come out of that bedroom. Time's a wasting."

Helen sighed and pulled herself off the bed where Skip's bathrobe was bunched up next to her pillow. She used it as a cuddle cushion because it still smelled like him. She didn't want to let go of it, but Wendy would nag her until she gave in.

"Just a minute, sweetie, I'm coming," she called back.

*   *   *

Helen had not planned to fall in love with the sea again, but she was fast losing that battle. Wendy wouldn't let her say no to another cruise, so she had to agree. Skip wouldn't like her moping about. That, she knew about him for sure.

The *Anthem of the Seas* cut through the sapphire waters of the Mediterranean as Helen stood at the rail, watching the Spanish coastline emerge from the morning mist. It was early May, and the air held that perfect warmth— not yet the scorching heat of summer, but pleasantly mild with temperatures in the low 70s.

"You going to stand there all day, or are you coming to breakfast?" Wendy appeared beside her, already dressed in a vibrant coral linen shirt and wide-brimmed hat.

Helen smiled. It was the first trip since the ill-fated voyage with Skip, her beloved husband. Sicily had been their last port together before everything changed— before the pandemic trapped them there, before the heart attack that knocked him flat on the street as he struggled with their luggage. She'd sworn she'd never set foot on another cruise ship. She was sure the reminder would have been too painful, but here she was again, embarking on an adventure with a friend.

Wendy had worn her down with persistent phone calls and finally showing up at her door with brochures. "Helen, baby, you're 66 years old, not 106. Skip wouldn't want you sitting in that house talking to his photograph.

Remember what he always said, getting comfortable is boring."

Helen sighed, "You're right. I feel like I need to have more discipline."

"Discipline is not what you need right now, my dear. Letting go is what you need, taking a chance on new vistas and sights and smells to pump some gas into that jalopy and turn back into a sports car."

Helen burst out laughing. "You have a way with words, Wendy. What do you have in mind?"

Helen had finally agreed. Wendy handled all the arrangements, a welcome relief for Helen who was used to running several businesses. But since Skip was no longer there to help her, she had lost her will to move forward.

And she was exhausted from the pain meds from her illness. That was something she didn't like to talk about. Everyone had something going on and hers was no worse than a lot of people's problems but the opioids for the pain left her in a depressed state. She had to get back on her maple syrup detox for a couple of days. It always helped lift her spirits. Her whole vibe was better when she was moving. Going to physical therapy made her stronger, and it helped silence some of the noise filling her head with, *what ifs and why didn't I see it coming, and what could I have done differently?*

* * *

The trip was turning out to be just what Helen needed. The ship was beautiful, and not too touristy or loud. She turned to her friend and said, "What's on the menu?"

After a relaxing breakfast on the aft deck of the beautiful Royal Caribbean cruise ship, Helen and Wendy planned their itinerary.

Barcelona, Spain was the first stop.

Gaudí's fantastical architecture spiraling into cloudless skies, greeted them with an awe inspiring respect for his amazing architectural imagination. Helen couldn't even imagine something like this getting through the planning board of any city council. It made her laugh to think of the arguments that would stop such a wonder in its tracks. They wandered through the Gothic Quarter, where Wendy insisted on stopping at every tapas bar. Helen found herself laughing—actually laughing— as Wendy attempted Spanish with wild hand gestures doing most of the talking, ordering patatas bravas and jamón ibérico (Iberian ham, with its rich, nutty flavor and marbled, melt-in-your-mouth texture) while flirting shamelessly with the handsome bemused waiter.

"See? You're still alive," Wendy said, squeezing her hand across the small table.

"Yeah..." replied Helen. "I was thinking today that I guess we are doing pretty good to be close to seventy. You can't believe it but it's true. I wish I could walk longer distances, but I am thankful that I can still walk and do a few things. Many women our age have knee replacements or hip replacement as well as carpal tunnel or high blood pressure or diabetes. That makes me grateful, and I am not very patient especially if I get anxious. My goal every day is to keep anxiety away."

Wendy reached out and gave her a hug. "You are right about all of that. I wake up every morning and say, Thank you Jesus, I am here for another day."

* * *

The weather was generous—sunny days with gentle breezes, occasional clouds that provided relief without threatening rain—perfect for walking.

In Valencia, they toured the futuristic City of Arts and Sciences, its white structures gleaming against the blue sky. Helen felt Skip's absence acutely here—he would have loved the architecture, would have taken a hundred photos. But she took her own photos, sending them to her son and daughter with messages that gradually grew longer, more animated.

Rome was overwhelming in the best way. The crowds at the Trevi Fountain, the majesty of the Colosseum, the humidity rising as May warmed the ancient stones. Wendy hired a driver who took them beyond the tourist sites to a family restaurant in Trastevere, where the owner's mother emerged from the kitchen to hug them both, insisting they try her cacio e pepe (Spaghetti With Black Pepper and Pecorino Romano).

"This is living, Helen," Wendy said, raising her wine glass as the late afternoon light turned golden on the verandah overlooking a river.

Helen saw the water glistening in the late afternoon glow. It was always water that made her remember the things that mattered most to her, her brother, her husband, her mother and father. There were so many people—friends and family—that she had lost, yet she was still here trying to make sense of it all.

But it was Naples that brought Helen's carefully maintained composure crumbling down. They were touring Pompeii under a warm sun, the temperature climbing into the upper 70s, when their guide mentioned that Pompeii was also a port town, a place where ancient Romans had come and gone on ships.

Helen had to sit down on a fallen column. Wendy dismissed the guide with a generous tip and sat beside her.

"It was two years ago this month," Helen said quietly. "We were supposed to come home. Instead, I came home alone."

Wendy didn't offer platitudes. She just sat there, her hand on Helen's back, as tourists streamed past.

"You know what Skip told me once?" Helen continued. "He said when he died, he wanted me to keep traveling. To see everything. He made me promise." She laughed bitterly. "I told him he was being morbid. We were only 62."

"So what do you want to do?" Wendy asked. "We can go back to the ship. We can go home early. Whatever you need."

Helen looked out over the ruins, at the shadow of Vesuvius in the distance, as the May sun warmed her face. She thought of Skip, of his laugh, of how he'd held her hand on the deck under the stars on that last night.

"I want gelato," she said finally. "The real stuff. And then I want to see the Amalfi Coast tomorrow like we planned."

The Amalfi Coast was breathtaking—dramatic cliffs plunging into turquoise waters, pastel villages clinging impossibly to the rocks. They took a boat to Capri, where the grottos gleamed with otherworldly blue light. The weather held perfect, warm but not hot, with a breeze that carried the scent of lemon groves. Helen breathed in the zesty aroma and felt a lightness she hadn't in years.

The two friends ate lunch perched on a terrace: *spaghetti alle vongole*, crusty bread, and chilled limoncello.

Then Wendy coaxed Helen to take a cliffside boat ride—waves lapping under the hull, foam fizzing like champagne. Helen dipped her hand into the water and threw the drops into the air. "Here's to you Joe," she whispered. She never, ever forgot her brother. He was her personal water sprite, keeping her grounded on what was important.

On their last evening aboard, as the ship sailed back toward Barcelona, Helen and Wendy sat on their balcony sharing a bottle of prosecco. The Mediterranean stretched endless and calm, reflecting the stars.

Helen took a sip. "I have dealt with tragedy quite a bit. So had Skip. So, our problem or our assignment was to learn how to overcome it and focus on the positive which we did as a team. We were definitely trauma bonded. I was more aware of his and not my own as are most black women. We acknowledge the challenging times for our men but not for ourselves. At this age I am finally getting more acquainted with myself—facing myself for the first time as an adult, with no one to lean on." she paused, "Except of course, you.

Wendy took a deep breath. "Same to you, my friend. I can always talk to you, share my deepest fears. And you can talk me down off me ledge, so to speak."

"I told my friend Gail that I have realized that there is much for me to learn about women who have gone through life with so much heartbreak if they continually have to handle life and remain feminine. I felt more powerful with Skip around me and did not want to do much without him. But this morning, God said to me loud and clear, "I am God and it's just you and me now, Helen. I know that's why I'm still here to get that together in my life. It's why Skip would say to me when I was in worry mode which was often, "You either have faith or you don't Helen."

"I would say of course I do BBUUTT. Haha. I'm learning now that I was still trying to figure out how we could or I could but not relying on God to accept the OUTCOME. Isn't that presumptuous? Asking God to not accept the outcome, because I was afraid?"

Wendy laughed out loud. "Helen, I never knew that's what you were worried about. I know you always over-thought things. That's when relying on GOD, no matter the outcome, has been where you needed to reside."

"I'm aware now," Helen said. "Better late than never. I need that peace because without it I can't function. I was in a highly operational crisis mode—fight or flight mode. Otherwise, I'm anemic. Truth 1000%? My energy came from adrenaline; from problems I must resolve or handle. Haha, no energy for that. Thank you," Helen said. "For not letting me give up. Your friendship has been a com-pass for me, a NorthStar so I never forget where I came from and where I belong."

"Girl, please. You were never going to give up. You just needed a push." Wendy clinked her glass against Helen's. "Besides, who else is going to keep me from get-ting arrested for public indecency when I inevitably go skinny dipping somewhere?"

Helen laughed—the deep, genuine laugh she thought she'd forgotten. "We're in our 60s, Wendy."

"Exactly. We've earned the right to do whatever the hell we want."

As the ship carried them through the night, Helen realized something had shifted. The grief was still there—it would always be there—but it no longer filled every space. There was room now for other things: for laughter, for new memories, for possibility.

Skip would have approved.

CHAPTER 11

A Life Well Lived

Helen knew she was made for this. That it was her assignment. That she didn't pick it. Her nephew who's a therapist said to her one day, "You know, Auntie, you deal with death a lot better than other people."

It's not anything that she really wanted to hang a trophy, all right. But it was just the truth. And then she thought about all this experience she had in helping others traverse this journey with their loved ones and even themselves when they knew death was coming.

She remembered this profound experience she had with a couple who were atheists. The man told her about his wife's mother dying in a bad boating accident. And he had been a Catholic. He asked Helen what she thought happened to her after death. Helen explained that she truly believe that his wife's mother graduated this life into another life and that would give her joy and peace. His wife was comforted. Because the mother and the son-in-law didn't get along, she came to him to tell him to tell his wife that she was okay. Helen felt her presence strongly and knew she was channeling the deceased for them.

The wife told Helen, "I was really upset about that."

Helen replied, "But you know what? He's supposed to take care of you. And it was emotional for you. So, she said it to him, because she knew he would be a comfort to you."

And then Helen asked her a question out of the blue, "Did you have an experience with your mother, prior to her passing?" Because it was an accident, according to them, and unexpected.

And she said, "Well, my mother had insisted that we go see *Phantom of the Opera* in New York."

Helen nodded her head and answered, "You know, souls know when they're leaving. And they'll do something later on to make you aware."

"Yeah, I see that now. Because I was in New York and Times Square, and I just got so happy. And I started crying. And I just felt like this is the best day ever. And two weeks later, my mother got killed. It was my mother who wanted me to remember that joy I felt when she sent us to New York."

Once those people experienced the miracle around the death of her mother, they couldn't be atheists any longer. Once you see the light you can't turn away.

Helen's Journal – Making Friends With Death

Souls don't travel in time like we do. Souls live forever is something most people don't even comprehend. Most people don't know the Bible at all. Jeremiah 1:5 signifies God's divine foreknowledge and purpose for individuals, stating, "Before I formed you in the womb I knew you."

In my experience, I have had those moments when almost everybody talks to me about death, and I got to the point where I could identify it and see things leading up to the event that was meant to be.

And that's where I just was. It never did make me feel better, like it wasn't just the way it was supposed to be.

A lot of people have faded out of my life. I know most of the time others are just in position for the lesson we need to learn and once learned they fade away.

Most of the time others are just props being in a position that triggers our responses. Once we conquer them the people aren't necessary in that way anymore. I'm less bothered in my brain but sometimes as a female my emotions make it more personal with others than it should be. I've had to rationalize my emotions with folks like my brother. I will start feeling distraught and then I catch myself and stop the sadness or worry and realize God's will is in effect as well and I need to calm myself down. It's Satan who wants to bring me down. It's a battle for sure.

The problem believing that the life here is all there is makes folks short-sided, fearful and childish essentially saying mine, mine, mine, me, me, me, and everyone else stinks. It is the dark side of human nature.

I have always felt I have a gift because most people have a very difficult time processing and dealing with death. They don't know how to deal with the anticipation of death and reality of death in the aftermath of death.

I've had many experiences with anticipatory grief of an expected death, death where you want people to leave because they're suffering, and accidental deaths that happen so suddenly it hits you like a brick. Then there is the most traumatic deaths like child death, baby death, ones that you really feel like a child was not supposed to leave right before you.

I would have had two sisters. My first sister died the same day she was born. My brother became a doctor and was doing his residency when his first son contacted cancer and died on his first birthday. So, there's been a lot of different layers of the way things happen, that also affect the way in which I have learned how to grow from these devastating experiences and help people understand.

I am grateful for the memories I have, and it sustains me greatly.

First, I would like to have children talking about it in a positive way and then keep them spiritually aware that they have a purpose while here. I think confronting it will make people live a more purposeful life. If someone dies, I hope it will stop all the meanness and fights that happen in families. When a transition occurs it's like a what-about-me fest instead of honoring and speaking on what they brought to each person, how they impacted their live. It shouldn't always be a cause for those left behind. Celebrating the journey is the biggest hope.

I'm hoping it will be what it needs to be. I want people to talk about transitions with more hope than dread. That's hard to do and accept grieving as well.

I'm burnt out after my parents, my siblings, and my Epps cousins required my constant assistance. I always cared, but the physical toll of the help they demanded, wore me out. I am done. Too much was expected because I always jumped in to help and they knew I know how to share.

My attitude is completely different, mainly because I can't do it anymore. I don't have the energy. I feel like I did that role enough in my life. Wendy has been one of the few who has constantly showed up. I appreciate that greatly. I think about it because my health is an ongoing part of my life that has to be honored at this point.

God told me that it was time for more self-reflection and now I'm doing what's best for me for a change.

My granddaughter would tell anybody who would listen, "My sister passed, just like she's my daughter," and I was really taken aback and she said, "Nana, you know, we all got to die."

But just trying to cope with it and hearing her say that already. It makes me also aware it's a gift that's being passed down, because she's already experiencing the truth, "You know, we're not going to die." My grandchildren are telling me angels are light. So, I know that they will be able to carry this on themselves. Because it's reality for us. It's our assignment to understand the cycles of life. Very few people are willing to work on this most important choosing.

Because what happened with my husband, and the people who knew me, started coming to me. There's no such thing as coincidence. I see everything and it kind of wears me out sometimes.

I have one more family member who's about to die. And that'll wipe out almost everybody at my house. So, when people ask how did I survive my whole group, even through my own personal health scares, I say because my journey was not done yet. I still go through days where I can't believe that I'm the last person standing from that generation.

But that's just because one thing you do learn from death is that we are just using this shell on a temporary basis. A lot of people like to pretend like the show is gonna go on forever. But if you really delve into the unknown, it transform you into a vessel of God. I had to learn that early in my life. When you don't consider that this not your only life, you might feel like you're a lot freer, but you're not. Because when you know when people are not going to be here, you do a lot of stuff differently.

* * *

Helen was in the hospital, nearing the final stage of her life. She had contributed so much to so many and changed people's lives. Her son and daughter were with her and some grandchildren and nieces. It was a gathering of the faithful. A smile lit up her face when she saw the children. She knew her legacy would carry on and she was ready to transition. Her granddaughter reached for her hand. "I can see you, Nana," she said. Helen started to say something, then stopped. She had nothing more to give, except one last soft breath. She had made friends with death a long time ago.

It was a few minutes before anyone realized she was gone, except her granddaughter.

"I can see you, Nana," she said again. Only this time was looking up to the ceiling were a soft white glow shown down on everyone in the room.

EPILOGUE

by
Lamar Vining

In the months after my mother died, I did not handle grief particularly well. I stayed busy solving problems and taking care of responsibilities, but I avoided sitting with the loss itself. I spent money impulsively, traveled more than usual, and found comfort in things that provided temporary pleasure—food, distractions, anything that filled the quiet space where grief tends to surface.

Ironically, all of that happened before I had truly read the book she had been writing about how to face death.

When I finally sat down and went through her words, something began to feel unmistakable.

The stories she told about helping families say goodbye…

The reflections she wrote about letting go…

The perspective she shared about finding peace in the presence of death…

It was as if she had unknowingly left behind a guide for the people who loved her most.

She wrote these pages for the world.

But in many ways, they first became a message to her son.

The lessons she spent years helping other families discover were the same lessons I needed in order to begin understanding my own loss.

My role in this book has simply been to make sure her voice reaches the people she hoped it would reach.

If you read this because you are facing the loss of someone you love—or because you know that one day you will—my hope is that the perspective she shared here brings you the same comfort it eventually brought me.

My mother believed that death is not the opposite of life. It is part of the same story.

Finishing this book helped me begin to understand what she meant. I hope it did the same for you.

Death Is Nothing At All

Henry Scott-Holland, 1847-1918

Death is nothing at all.
It does not count.
I have only slipped away into the next room.
Nothing has happened.

Everything remains exactly as it was.
I am I, and you are you,
and the old life that we lived so fondly together is
untouched, unchanged.
Whatever we were to each other, that we are still.

Call me by the old familiar name.
Speak of me in the easy way which you always used.
Put no difference into your tone.
Wear no forced air of solemnity or sorrow.

Laugh as we always laughed at the little jokes that we
enjoyed together.
Play, smile, think of me, pray for me.

Let my name be ever the household word that it
always was.
Let it be spoken without an effort, without the ghost of a
shadow upon it.

Life means all that it ever meant.
It is the same as it ever was.
There is absolute and unbroken continuity.
What is this death but a negligible accident?

Why should I be out of mind because I am out of sight?
I am but waiting for you, for an interval,
somewhere very near, just round the corner.

All is well.
Nothing is hurt; nothing is lost.
One brief moment and all will be as it was before.
How we shall laugh at the trouble of parting when we
meet again!

About Helen Vining

Helen Louise Epps was one of seven children She married the love of her life, Elmer Vining, on March 21, 1977. The couple was blessed with the birth of one son and one daughter.

While starting her career in human resources management, Helen demonstrated an entrepreneurial spirit which eventually led her to attain her bachelor's degree in finance which enabled her to establish her own CPA business. Many of her clients from the local community valued her integrity and commitment to their financial well-being, as much as they did her friendship.

Beyond her professional achievements, Helen held a deep appreciation for the world around her. Her love for travel became a lifelong passion that took her to the farthest corners of the globe. She was fascinated by cultures and landscapes as diverse as Egypt's ancient relics, the vibrant rhythms of the Dominican Republic, and the spiritual heart of the Vatican. Cruises to stunning locales like St. Lucia offered her further opportunities to explore and indulge her adventurous spirit. She cherished her time spent at Detroit's renowned cultural venues, such as the Fox Theatre and the Detroit Opera House, where she would often be seen dressed to the hilt, embracing the arts with enthusiasm.

Helen's heart was deeply rooted in her love for family. As a dedicated mother and grandmother, she was the cornerstone of her family. Her grandchildren were her pride and joy, and she showered them with love, and endless support. Known as the family's genealogist, she meticulously documented their history and stories, ensuring that the legacy of her family's past would be preserved for generations to come.

As her own generosity knew no bounds; she believed in helping others reach their potential, and often quietly paid for the college education of those in need, offering them a future full of promise.